THE
LOW G STRING TUNING
UKULELE

by Ron Middlebrook

Ukulele played and recorded with thanks to Steve Barden

ISBN 978-1-57424-269-0
SAN 683-8022

Cover by James Creative Group

The Ukulele

The Ukulele, the most charming and favorite of all Hawaiian musical instruments, is made out of koa or kou, a wood that is rare and valued greatly by the Hawaiians. The shape is that of a very small guitar, but strung with only four strings. The Hawaiians have a way of playing over all the strings at the same time, strumming and skipping their fingers from one side of the instrument to the other, hence the name, Ukulele, (a bouncing flea).

The instrument is used greatly in accompanying songs and, especially with the Hawaiian songs, the effect is very brilliant and fascinating, and any quintet, glee or musical club in the islands, without the Ukulele, is far from being perfect. It is as needful to any Hawaiian quintet club as a snare drum is to a military brass band.

Some would call the Ukulele an insignificant instrument, and yet we have all there is necessary to make and cover an accompaniment for the most difficult opera written, the harmony is all there, if one would give it a complete and thorough study.

Of course, with proper instruction, one could easily become a clever performer in a very short time, and in a few lessons; but that is not to say that any one could acquire all there is required of the instrument in a short time. And, one who is learning, can have more pleasure out of an Ukulele in one month than he could on a guitar or any stringed instrument in a year.

Ernest K. Kaai. 1910

Ernest K. Kaai (bottom center)

Contents and CD track list

To get the most out of this book, you'll want to replace the fourth (high G) string with one of a heavier gauge and tune it an octave lower to get that full deep sound in playing the melodies in this book. The chords can be played with or without the low G string.

Your local music store should be able to help you in attaining the proper string gauge for your soprano, concert or tenor ukulele.

The recommended string gauge is: soprano/concert 0.26, 0.28 or .032. tenor .032.

Several string brands sell sets with the low g string. Here are a few brands to check out: "Kala Red"- low wound G, "Ko'olau Mahana" Tenor ukulele low G strings with wound third and fourth strings.

Jesse Kalima

Jesse Kalima (1920-1980)

   Jesse Kalima was born in Honolulu in 1920, at a time when the ukulele was just becoming recognized for its capability to be played as a solo instrument. At age 15, Kalima burst into the public music scene, and established himself as the man credited with accelerating the development of the solo ukulele, when he won the Hawaii amateur ukulele championship by playing the march "Stars and Stripes Forever". This march became an instant hit, and has for many years been a goal of young ukulele players developing their solo skills,

   Kalima, a self-taught musician, developed innovative techniques for his solo style. As a result of his quest for a more full deep sound, he popularized the tenor ukulele, as well as a modified tuning where the forth string is lowered by one octave. He was also Hawaii's ukulele virtuoso. In 1938, he organized the Kalima Brothers band with three members of his family, who became known later as 'A Thousand Pounds of Melody". During World War II and the immediate post-war period, the Kalimas played at USO shows and at clubs all over the islands. At this time, Kalima was the biggest name in ukulele. The band's many recordings became best sellers. Many friends and family members were part of the band over the years, including Kalima's sons Jesse Jr. and Dana. Jesse also manufactured his own line of ukuleles. (The Ukulele Hall of Fame Museum)

Trader Vic's Night Club
Jesse Kalima, Junior Kalima, Henry Mucha, Honey Kalima, Albert Kalima

Amazing Grace

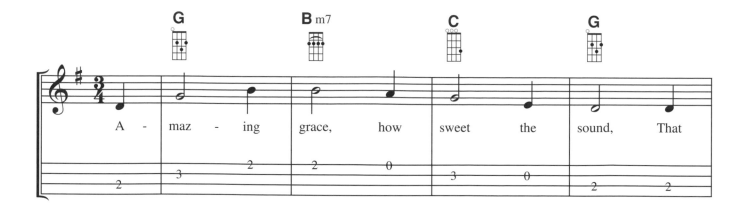

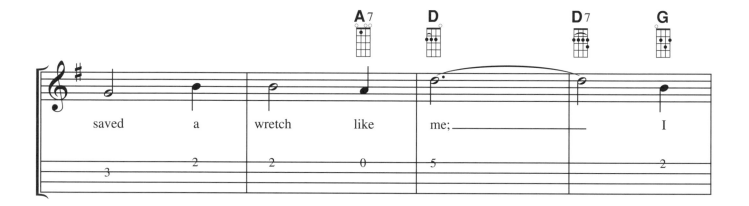

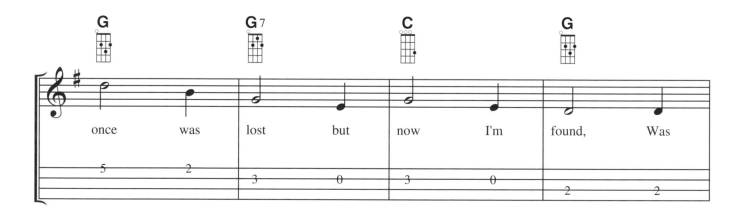

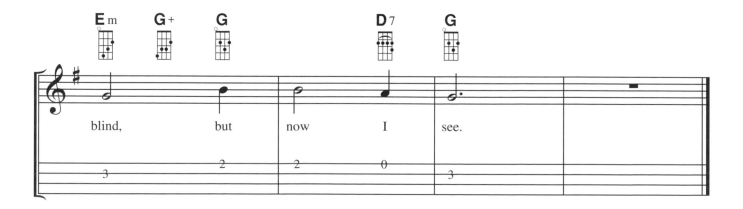

America

(My Country 'Tis Of Thee)

P = Pull off

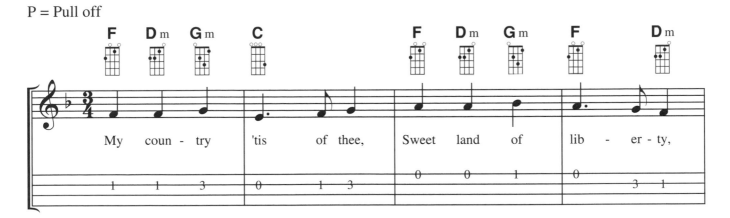

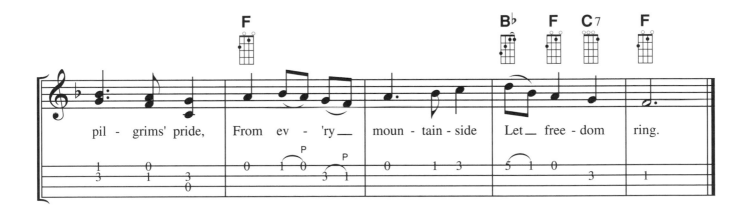

The Battle Hymn of the Republic

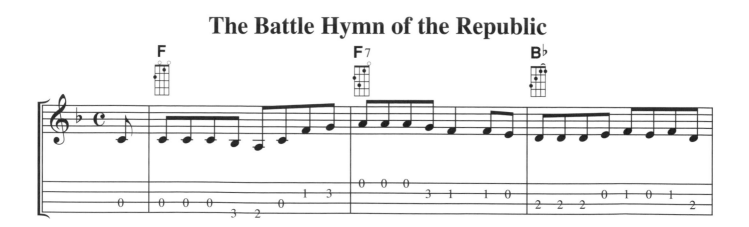

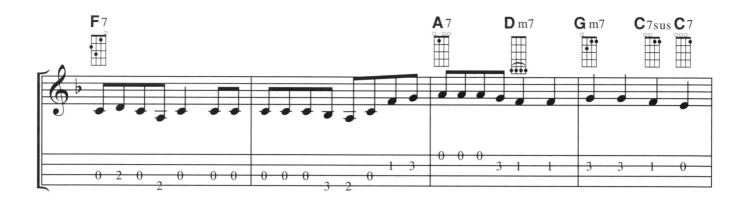

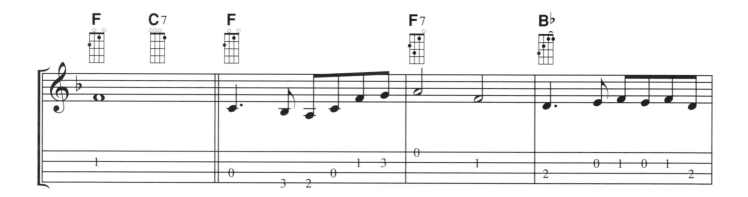

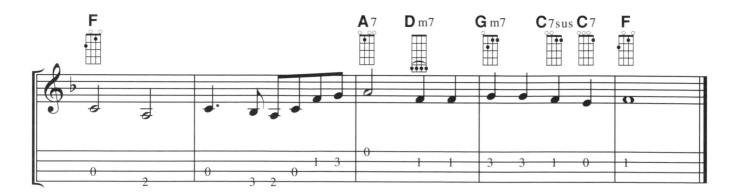

The Big Rock Candy Mountain

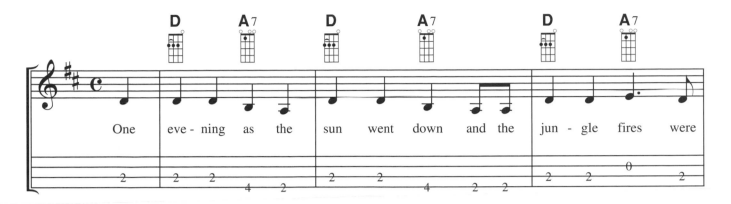

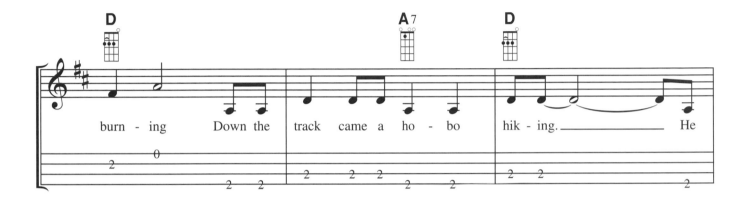

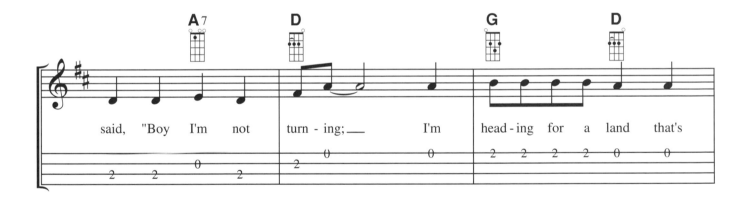

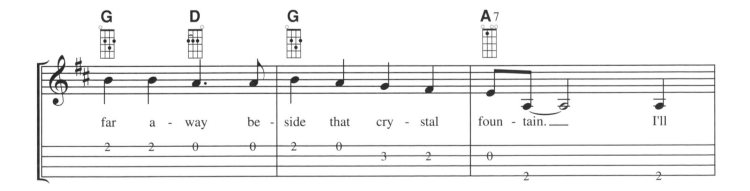

This arrangement copyright by Centerstream Publishing llc

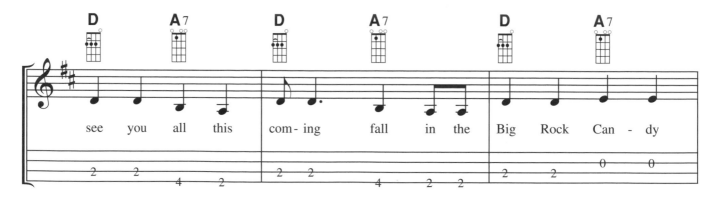

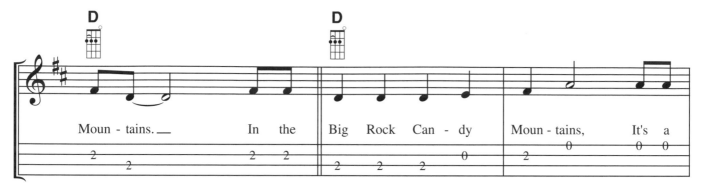

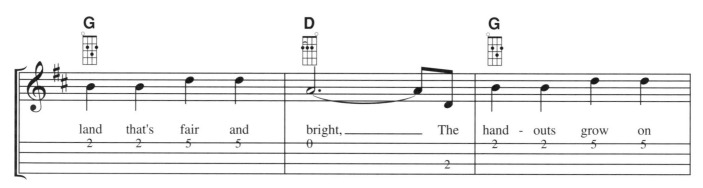

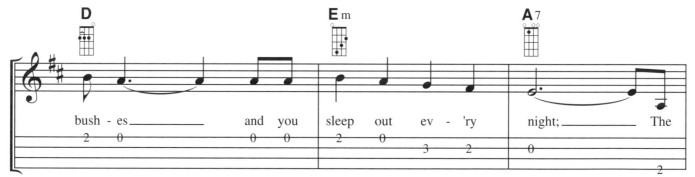

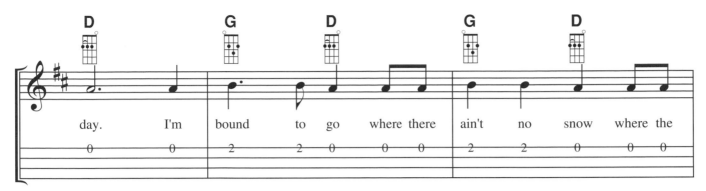

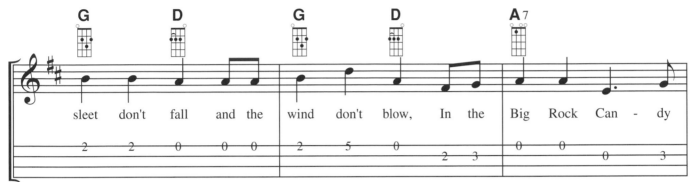

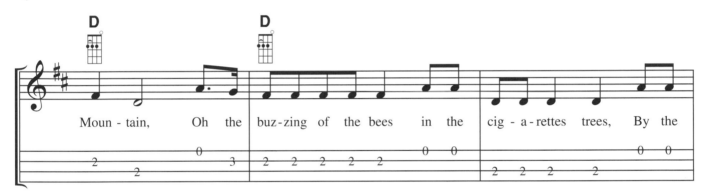

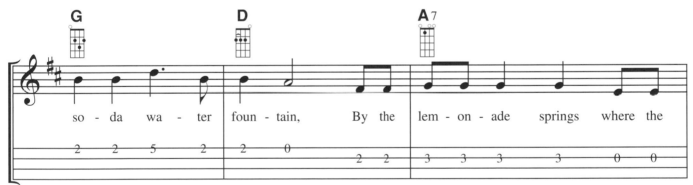

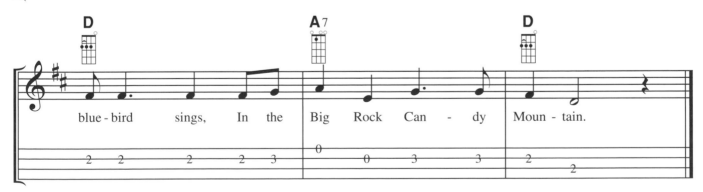

Cindy

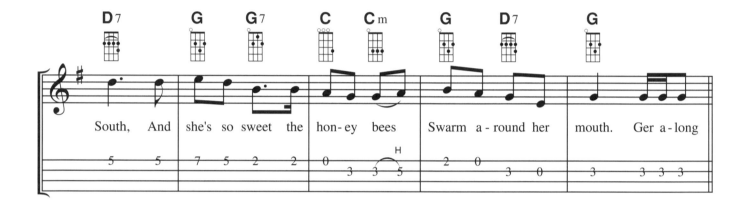

Chorus

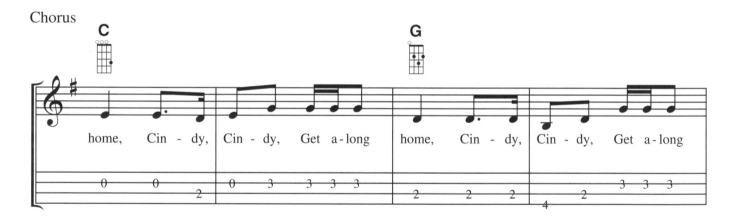

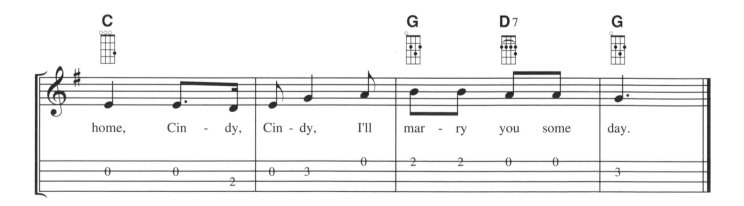

For Me And My Gal

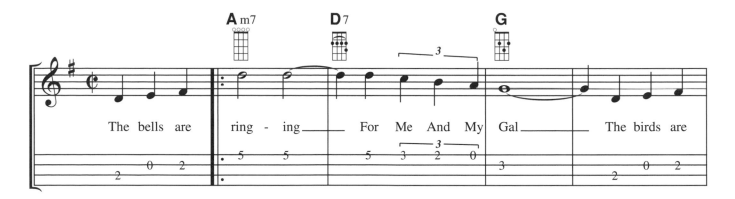

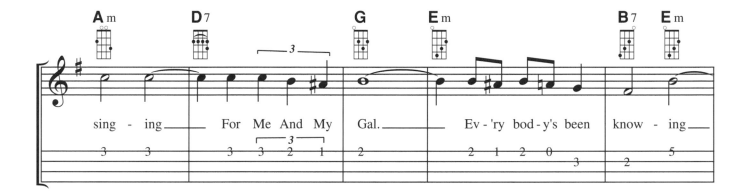

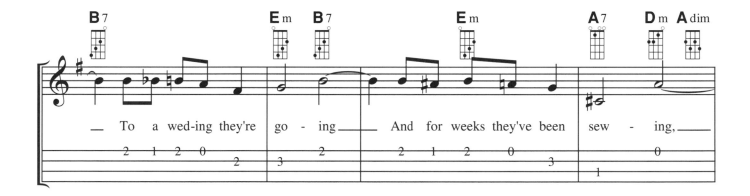

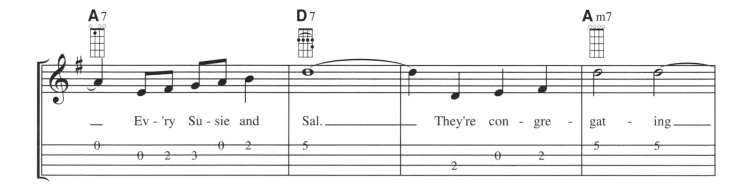

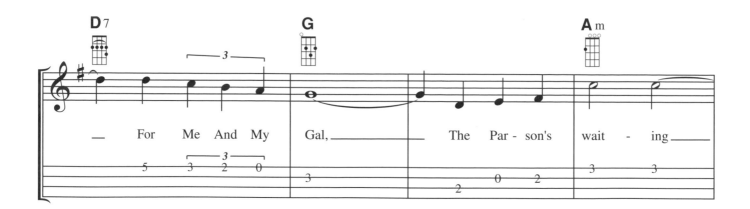

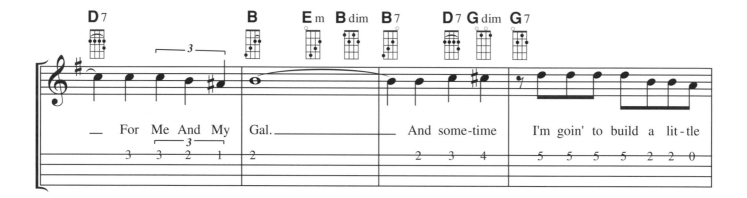

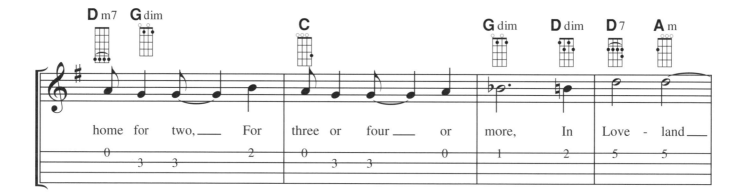

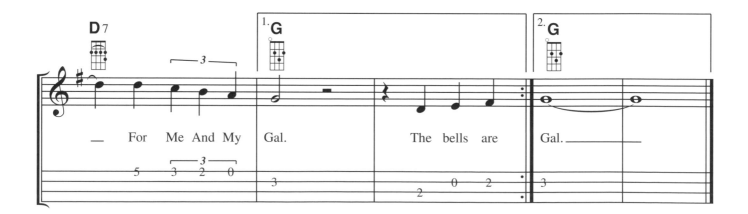

Cliff Edwards recorded "Singing in the Rain", September, 23 1929. Singing this song in the 1929 movie "Hollywood Revue" became a smash success. Cliff Edwards will always be remembered as the voice of Jiminy Cricket in Walt Disney's classic "Pinocchio" cartoon. Cliff sang the Oscar award winning song, "When You Wish Upon A Star" that has become a standard and the theme song for various Disney projects around the world. Of course we all know Cliff by his nickname "Ukulele Ike".

A Good Man Is Hard To Find

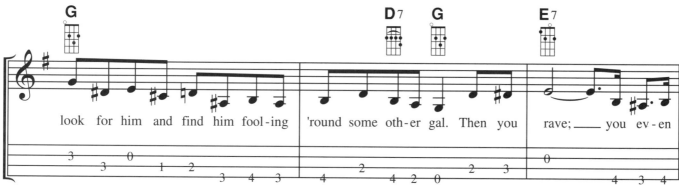

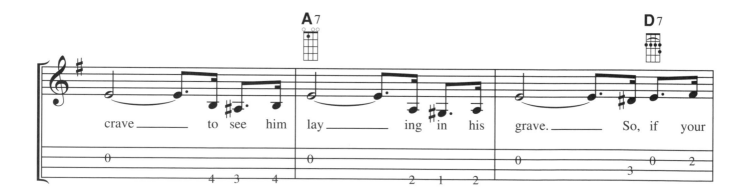

16

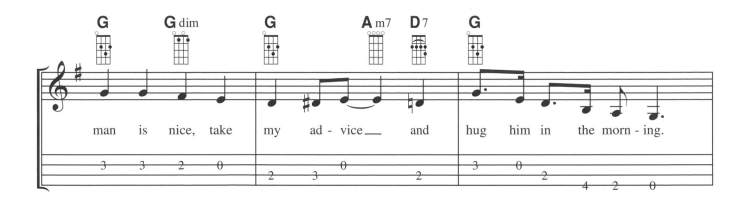

man is nice, take my ad-vice ___ and hug him in the morn-ing.

Kiss him ev-'ry night. ___ Give him plen-ty lov-in', treat him right ___ for a

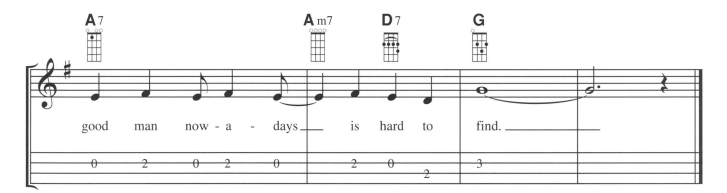

good man now-a-days ___ is hard to find. _____

Grandfather's Clock

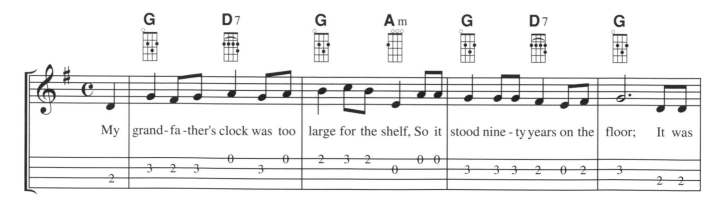

My | grand-fa-ther's clock was too | large for the shelf, So it | stood nine - ty years on the | floor; It was

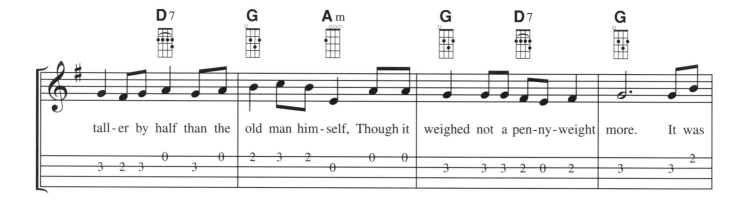

tall - er by half than the | old man him - self, Though it | weighed not a pen-ny-weight | more. It was

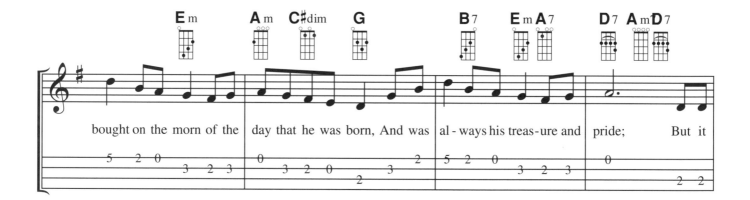

bought on the morn of the | day that he was born, And was | al - ways his treas-ure and | pride; But it

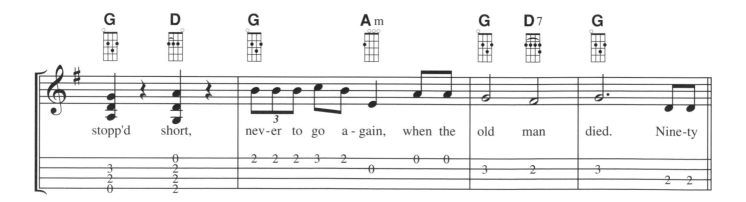

stopp'd short, | nev-er to go a-gain, when the | old man died. Nine-ty

Chorus

years with-out slum-ber-ing, tick, tock, tick, tock, His life se-conds num-ber-ing, tick, tock, tick, tock, It

stopp'd short, nev-er to go a-gain, when the old man died.

19

He Aloha No Kauiki
(A Love For Flowers)

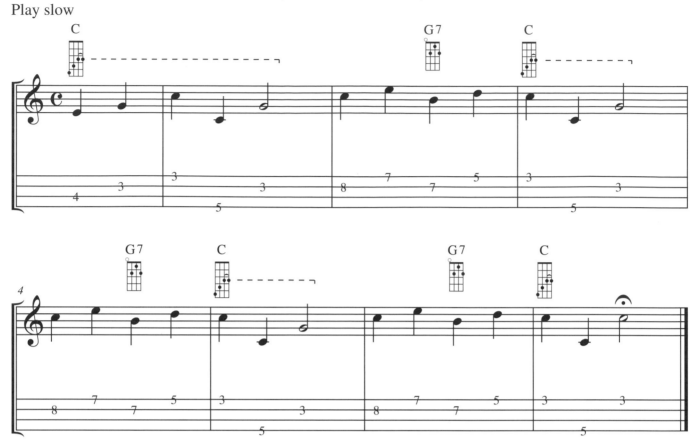

Ernest Kaleihoku Kaai (1881-1962)

Ernest Kaai, arguably the most influential musical figure in Hawaii in the first quarter of the 20th century, was a gifted performer on many instruments including the mandolin, guitar and ukulele. He was also an impresario, teacher, recording artist and published his first ukulele instructional book in 1906. Known in Honolulu as the "Father of the Ukulele", Kaai was said to have been the first musician to play a complete melody with chords. He promoted the ukulele as a featured instrument in the Hawaiian orchestra, his sophisticated finger, picking and stroke styles also inspired the modern establishment of the ukulele as a solo instrument. He also owned the Kaai Ukulele Manufacturing Company, advertised from 1909-1920. Sold it in 1917and became a shareholder in the newly formed Aloha Ukulele Manufacturing Company. Kaai left Hawaii in 1923 to tour the Far East and Australia, and eventually settled in Sri Lanka. In the mid-1930s, he planned to open a "Hawaiian Village" in Shanghai, China, but the war forced him to flee and he returned to Hawaii in 1937. He moved to Miami, Florida, in 1941 and incorporated the Kaai Music Studios in 1946. He died in Miami in 1962. (The Ukulele Hall of Fame Museum)

Ernest Kaai, circa 1917, Ukulele Hall of Fame Museum

Hi'ilawe
(To Lift or to Carry)

H = hammer on
P = pull off

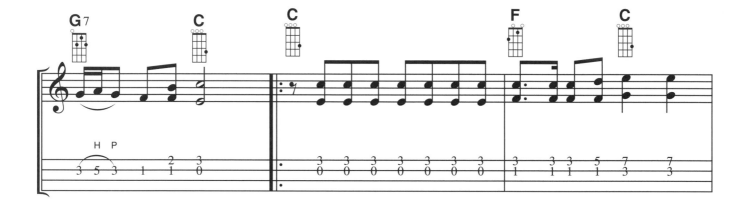

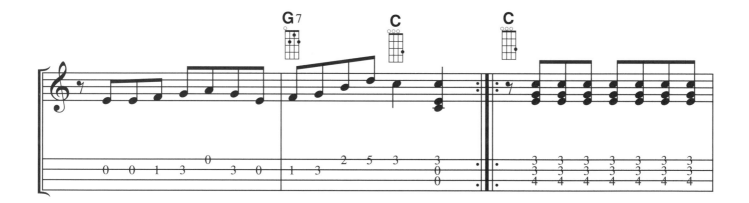

22

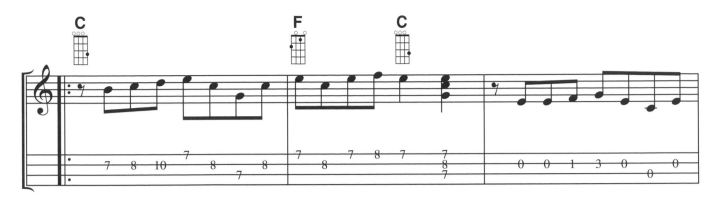

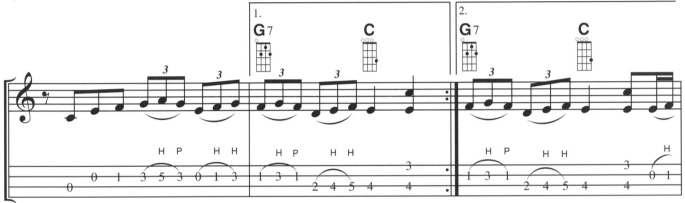

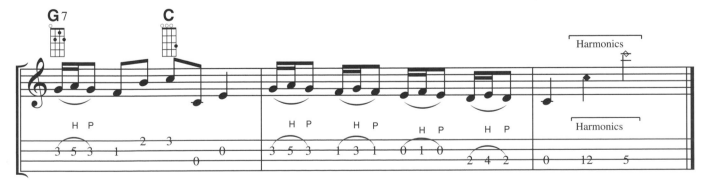

23

Honesakala
(Honeysuckle)

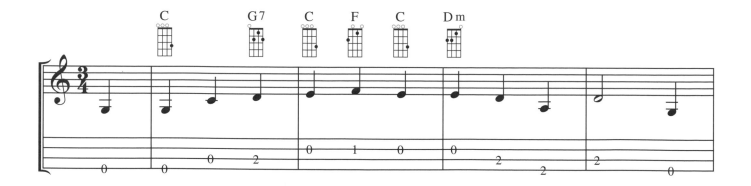

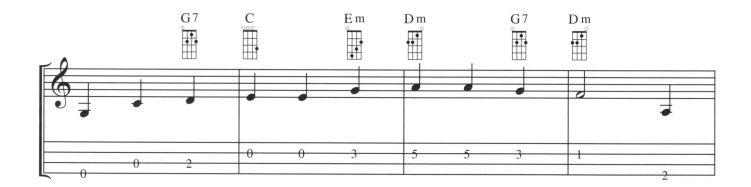

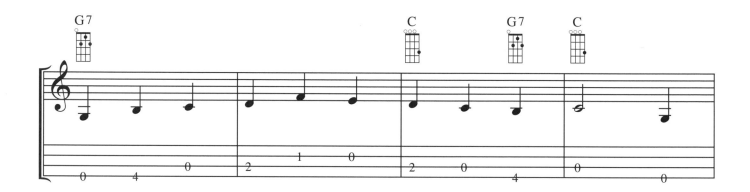

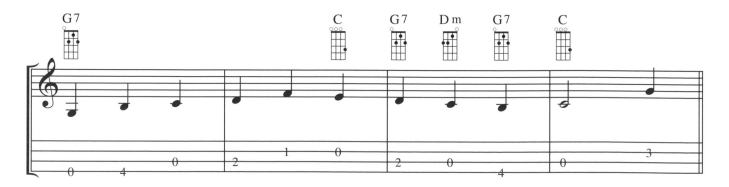

Try a little syncopation for this part

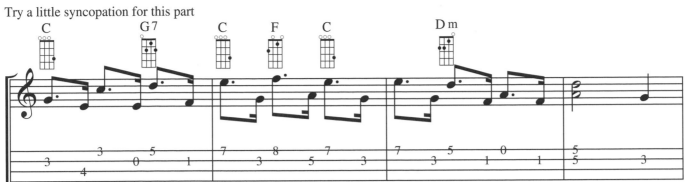

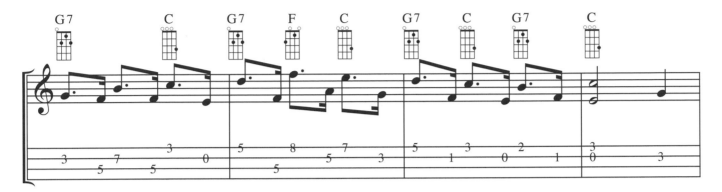

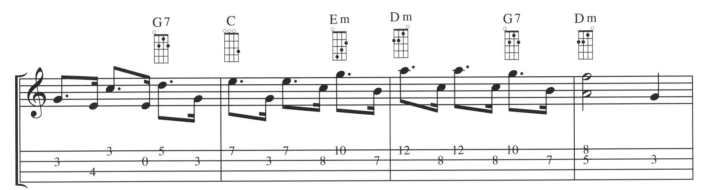

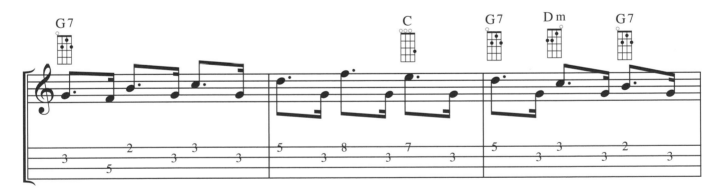

Kuu Ipo I Ka Hee Pue One
Ipo means sweetheart in Hawaiian

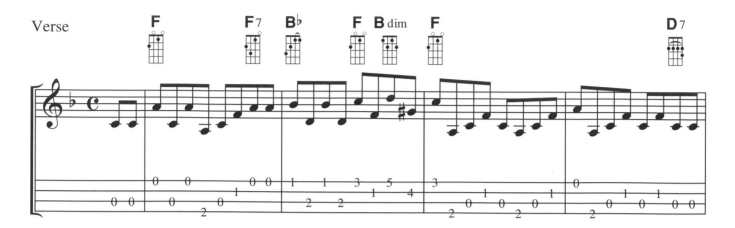

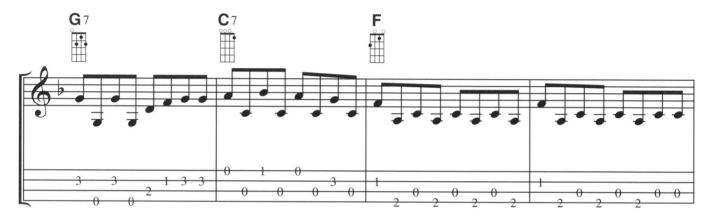

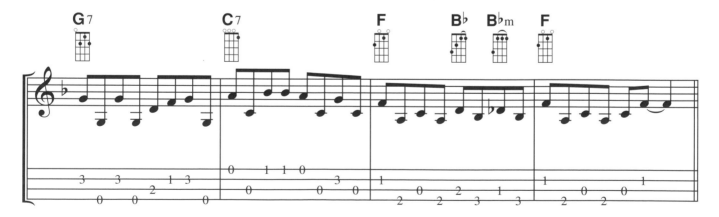

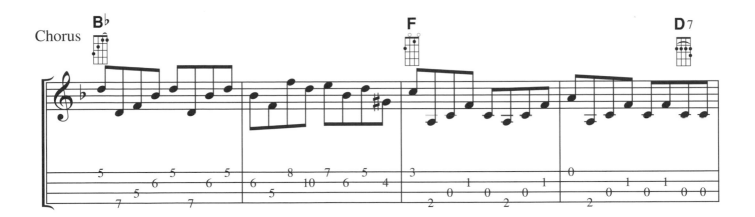

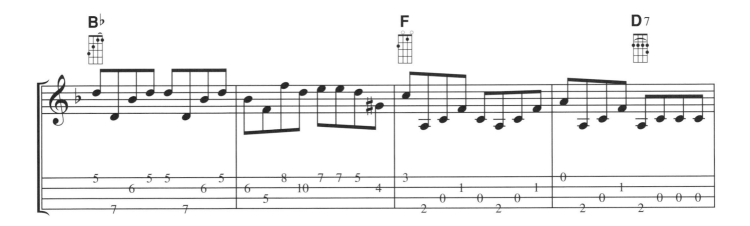

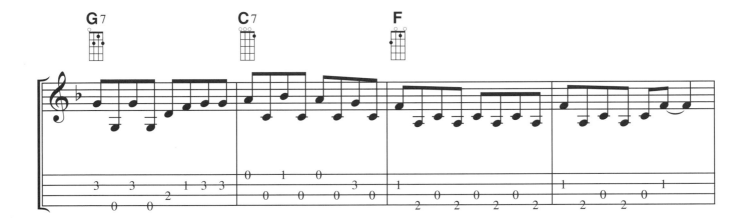

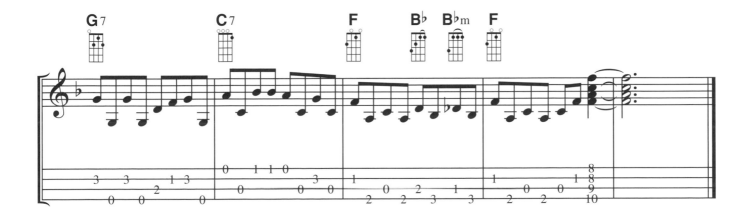

Little Brown Jug

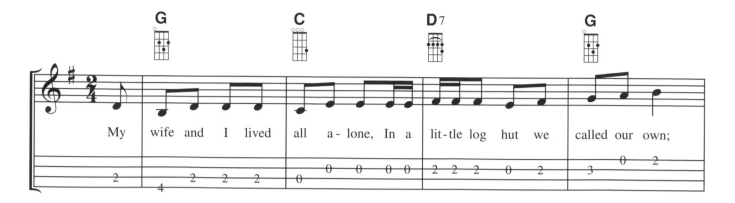

My wife and I lived all a-lone, In a lit-tle log hut we called our own;

She loved gin and I loved rum, I tell you we had lots of fun.

Chorus

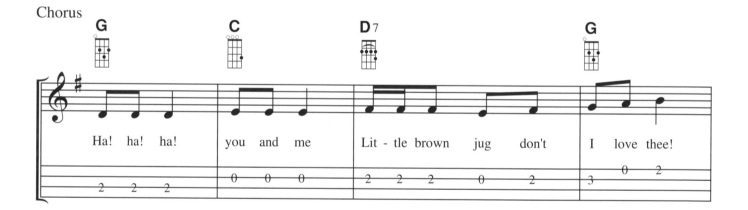

Ha! ha! ha! you and me Lit-tle brown jug don't I love thee!

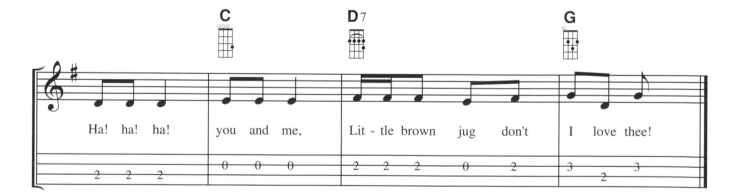

Ha! ha! ha! you and me, Lit-tle brown jug don't I love thee!

Manuela Boy
(Manuela is a Portuquese name for a man)

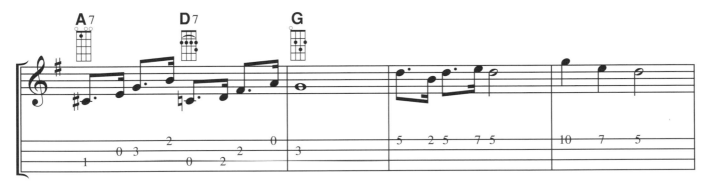

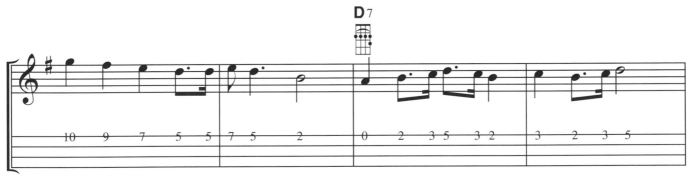

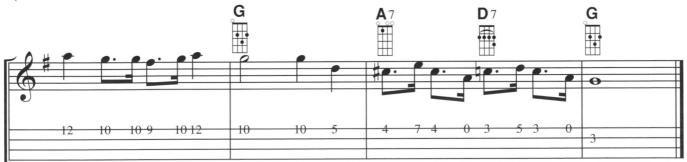

The Marine's Hymn

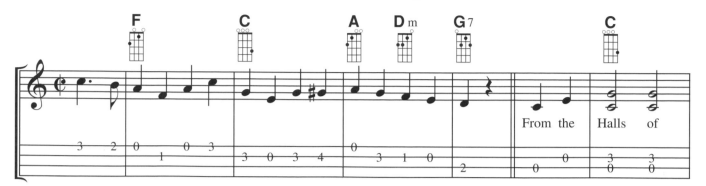

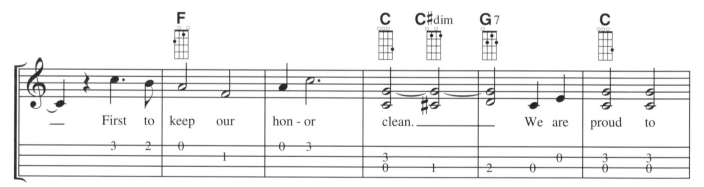

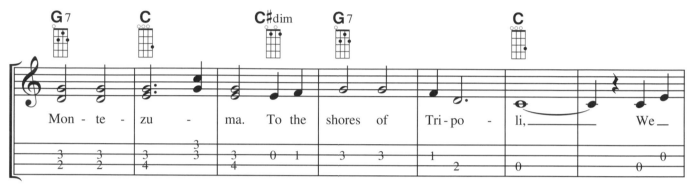

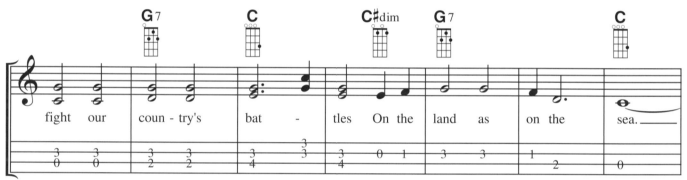

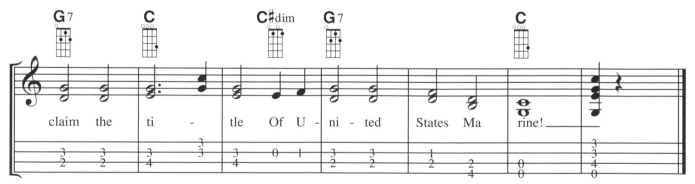

This arrangement copyright by Centerstream Publishing llc

Maui No Ka O

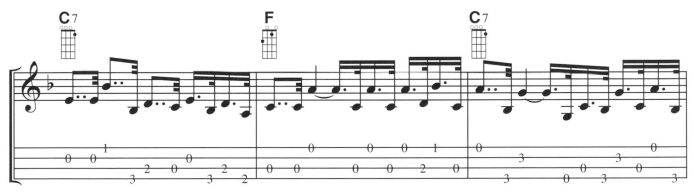

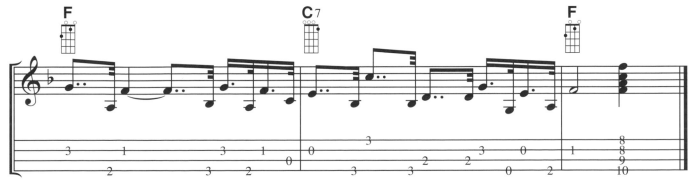

My Honolulu Hula Girl

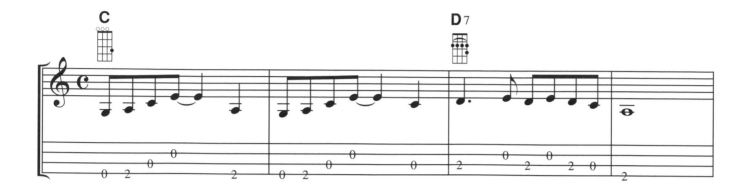

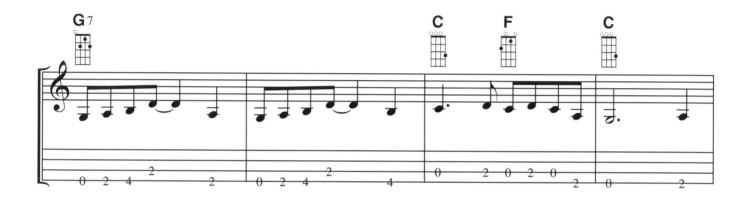

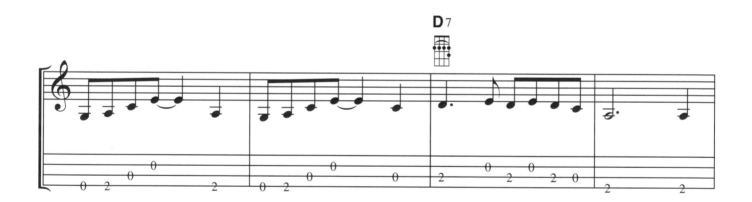

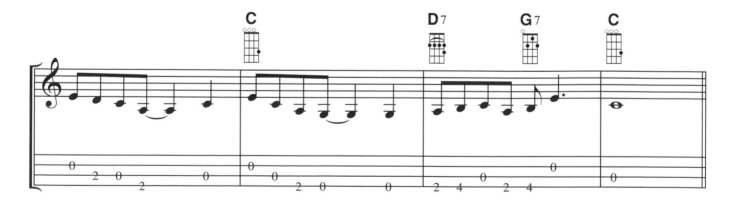

2

My Honolulu Hula Girl

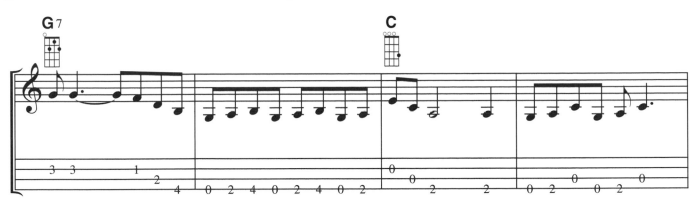

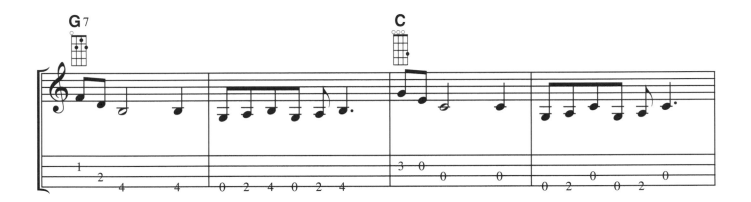

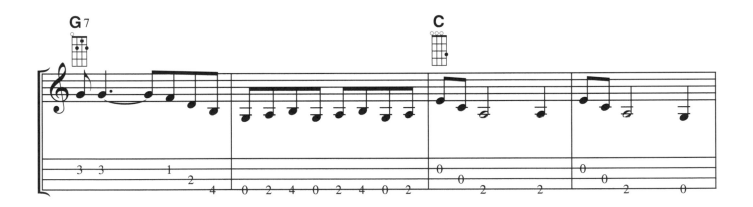

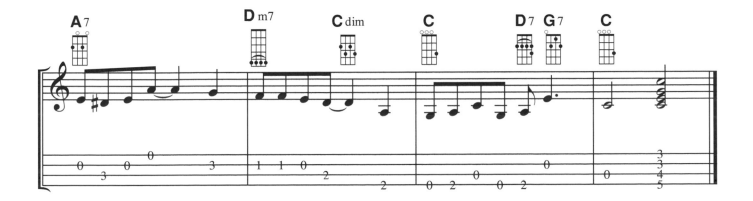

Over There

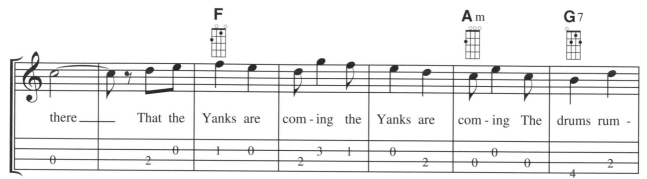

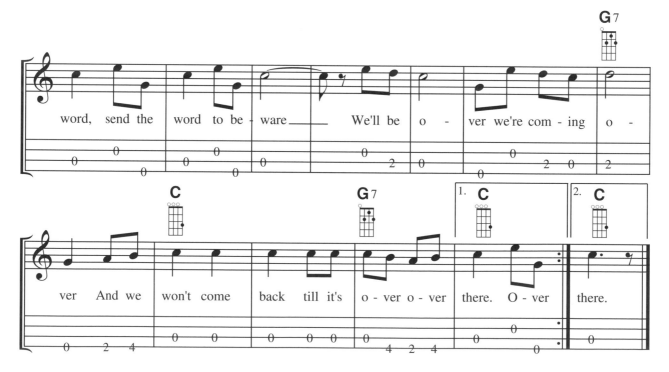

The Star Spangled Banner

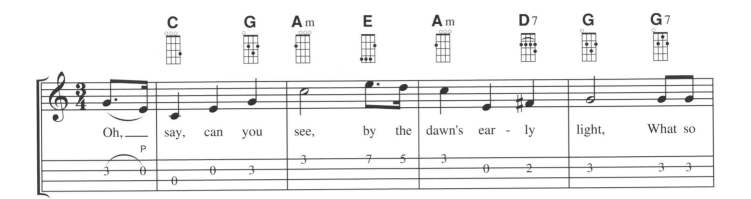

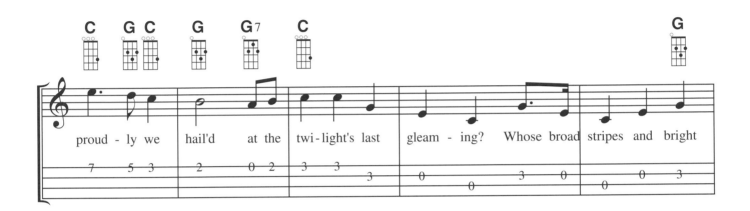

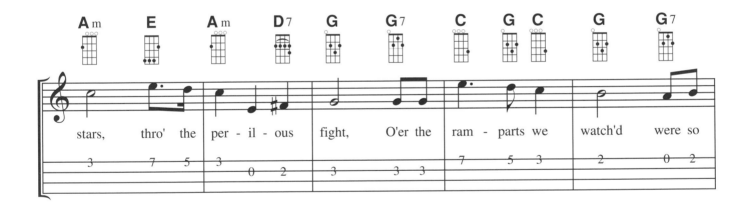

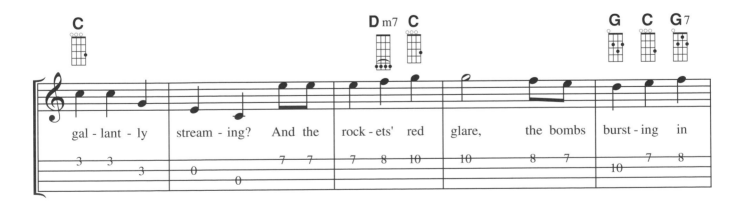

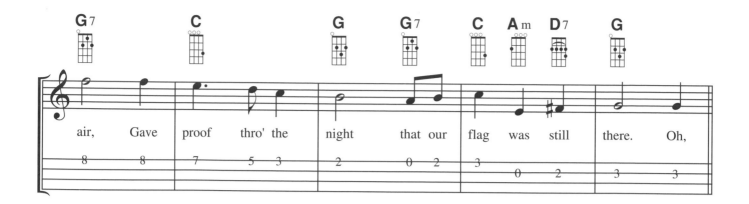

air, Gave proof thro' the night that our flag was still there. Oh,

Chorus

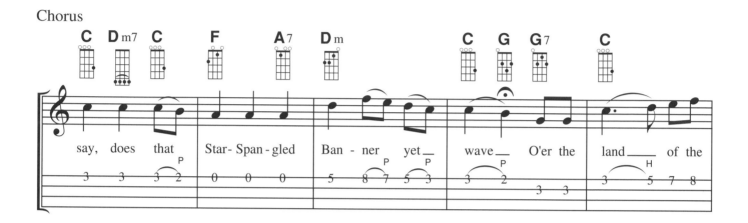

say, does that Star- Span - gled Ban - ner yet wave O'er the land of the

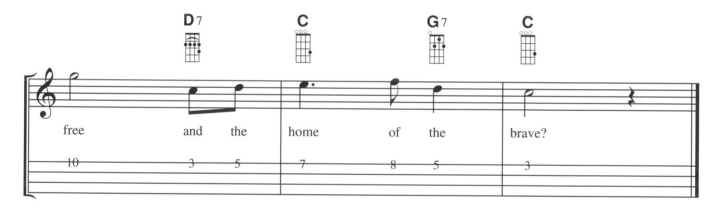

free and the home of the brave?

Sunny Manoa

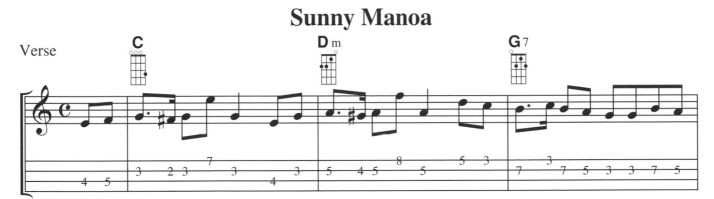

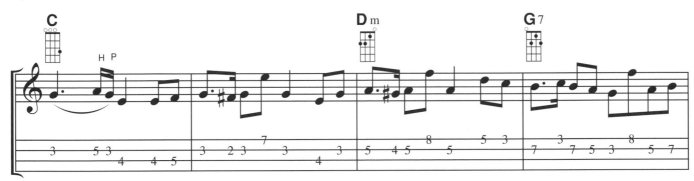

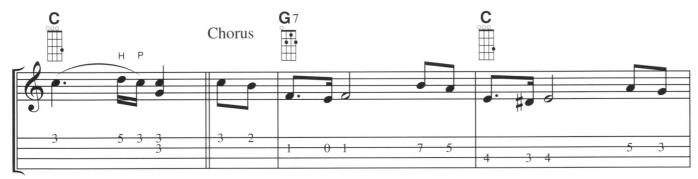

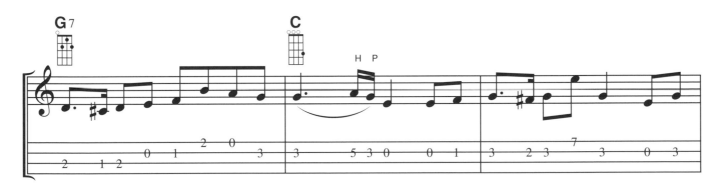

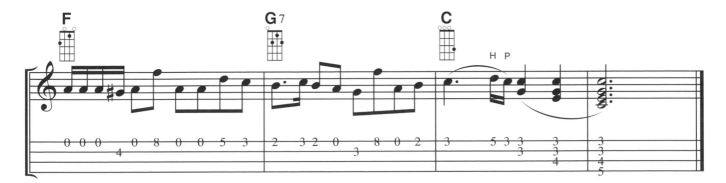

St. Louis Blues

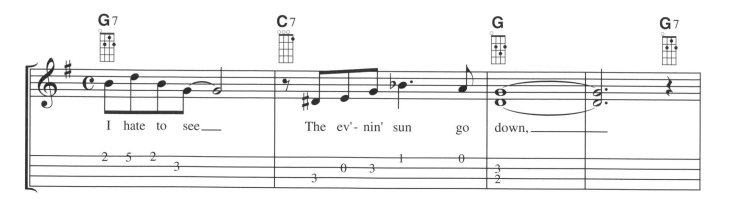

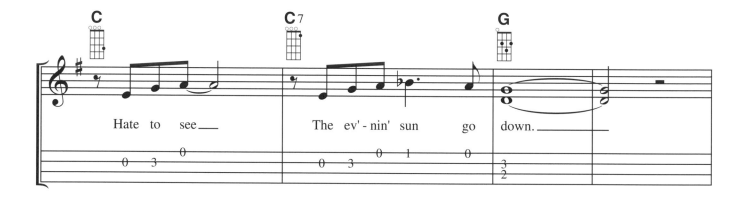

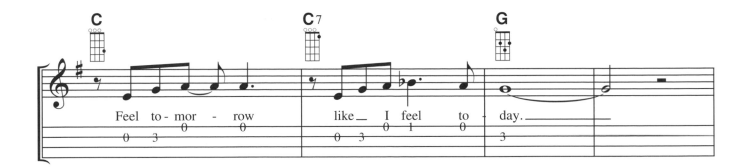

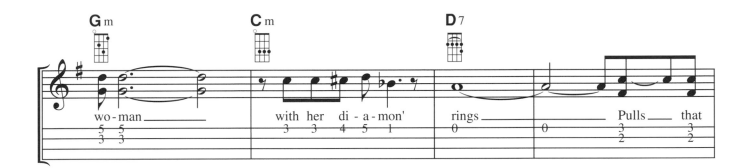

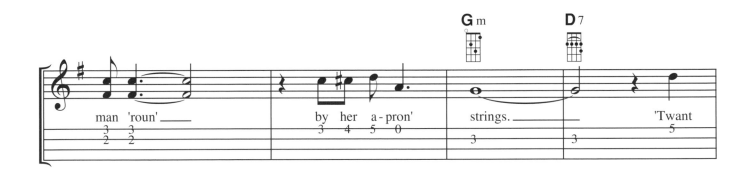

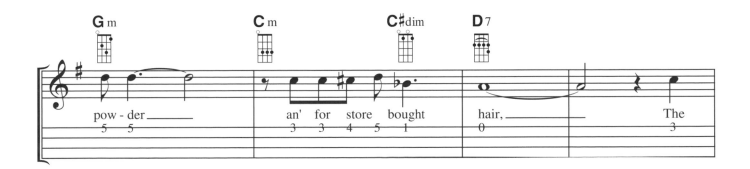

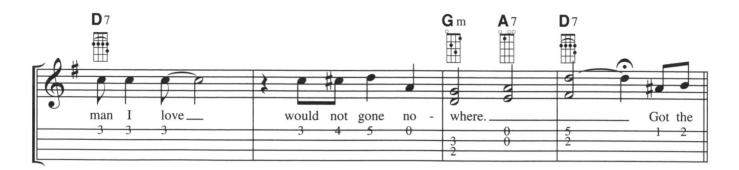

Chorus

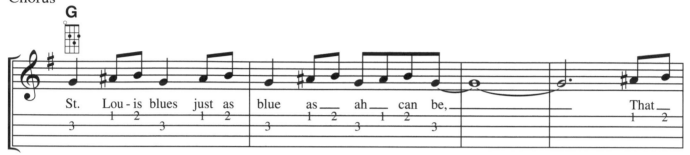

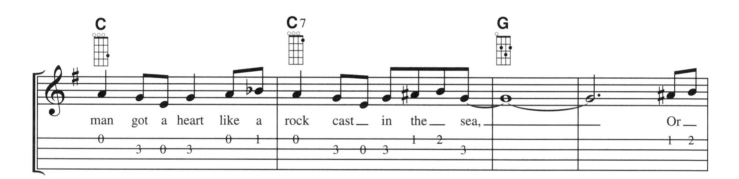

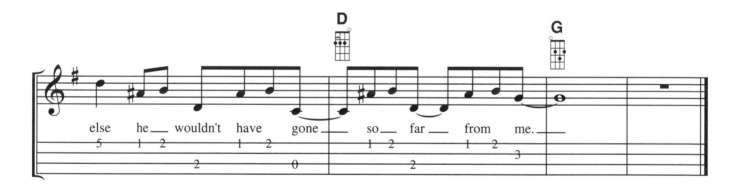

Take Me Out to the Ball Game

In 1858, the first known baseball song was written, "The Base Ball Polka!" It was not quite as famous as Jack Norworth's 1908 classic, "Take Me Out to the Ball Game", a poem which was written on some scrap paper on a train ride to Manhattan, New York when he spotted a sign that said "Ballgame Today at the Polo Grounds." Norworth then provided those paper scrap lyrics to Albert Von Tilzer who composed the music that in turn was published by the York Music Company and before the year was over, a hit song was born. An interesting note, it's said that neither Norworth or Tilzer had ever been to baseball game at the time the song was written.

Jack Norworth was a very successful vaudeville entertainer-songwriter and spent fifteen minutes writing this classic that is sung during the seventh inning stretch at early every ballpark in the country. In 1927, he changed some lyrics and a second version appeared.

1908 Version
Katie Casey was baseball mad,
Had the fever and had it bad.
Just to root for the home town crew,
Ev'ry sou˙ Katie blew.
On a Saturday her young beau
Called to see if she'd like to go
To see a show, but Miss Kate said "No
I'll tell you what you can do".

[Chorus]
    Take me out to the ball game,
    Take me out with the crowd;
    Buy me some peanuts and Cracker Jack,
    I don't care if I never get back.
    Let me root, root, root for the home team,
    If they don't win, it's a shame.
    For it's one, two, three strikes, you're out,
    At the old ball game.

Katie Casey saw all the games,
Knew the players by their first names.
Told the umpire he was wrong,
All along, Good and strong.
When the score was just two to two,
Katie Casey knew what to do,
Just to cheer up the boys she knew,
She made the gang sing this song:

    *The term "sou", now obscure,was at the
    time common slang for a low-denomination coin.

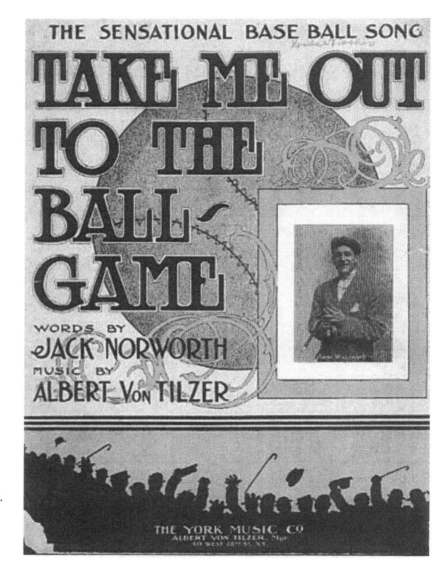

Take Me Out To The Ball Game

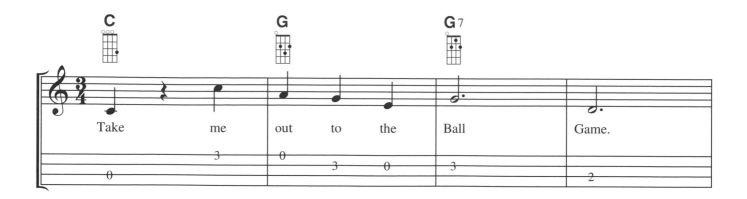

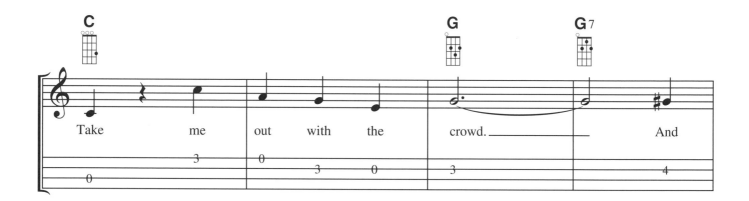

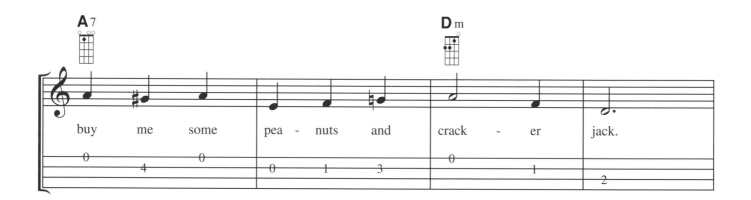

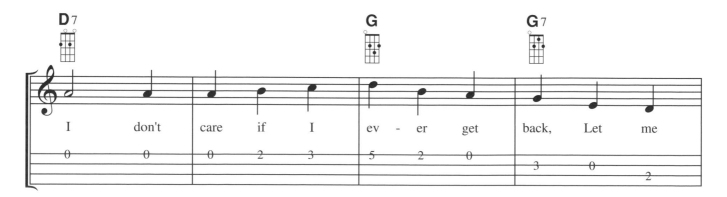

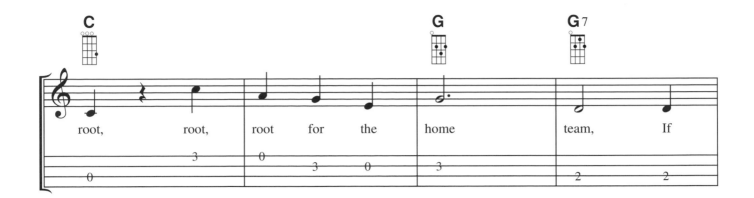

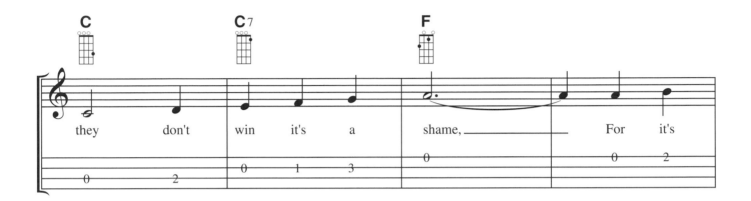

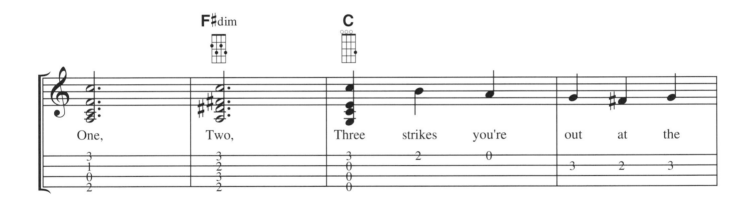

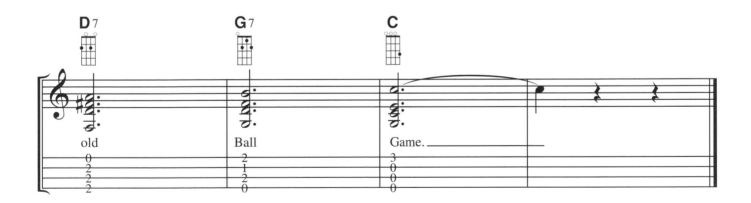

When The Saints Come Marching In

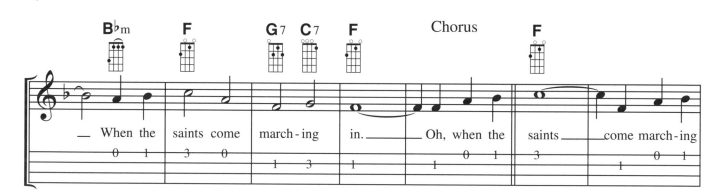

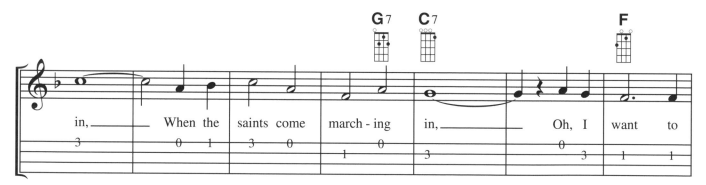

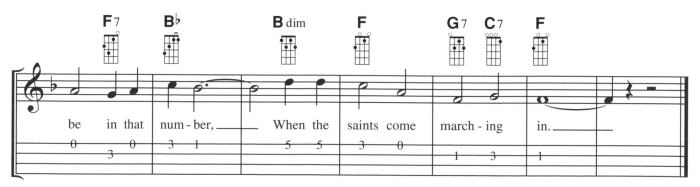

Wildwood Flower

I will   twine   and will   min - gle   my   ra - ven black

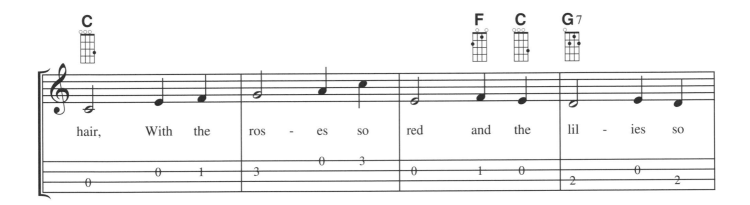

hair,   With   the   ros - es   so   red   and   the   lil - ies   so

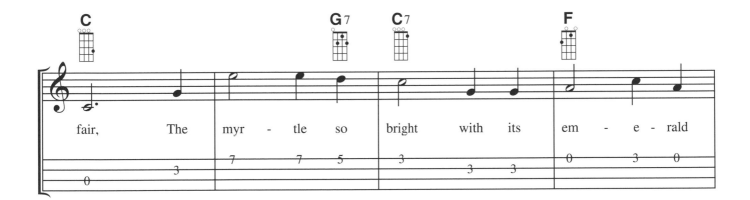

fair,   The   myr - tle   so   bright   with   its   em - e - rald

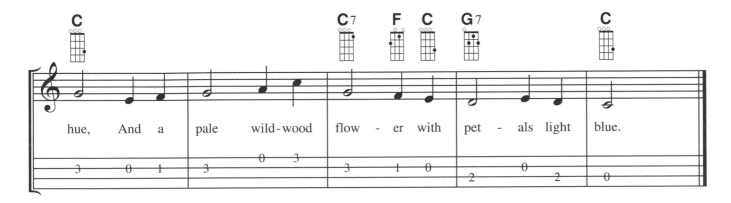

hue,   And   a   pale   wild - wood   flow - er   with   pet - als light   blue.

Yankee Doodle

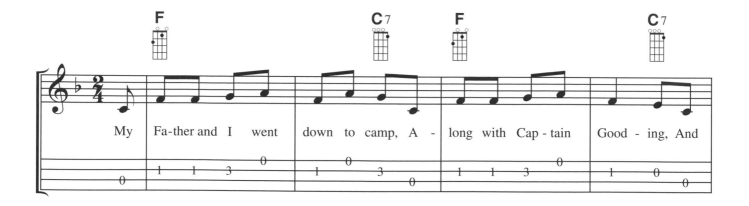

Chorus

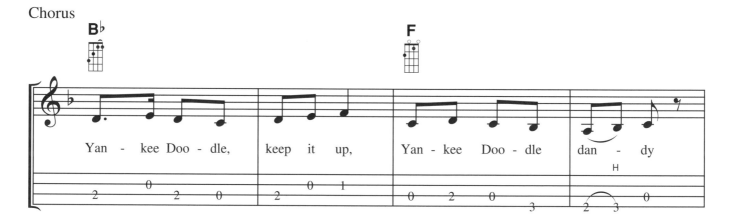

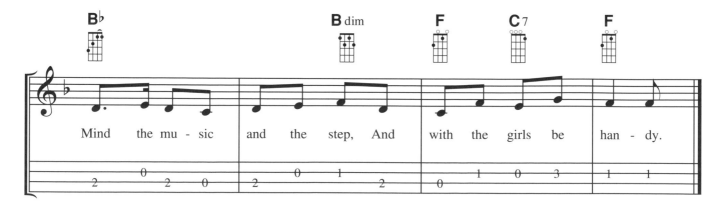

This arrangement copyright by Centerstream Publishing llc

More Great Books from Centerstream...

CHRISTMAS UKULELE, HAWAIIAN STYLE

Play your favorite Christmas songs Hawaiian style with expert uke player Chika Nagata. This book/CD pack includes 12 songs, each played 3 times: the first and third time with the melody, the second time without the melody so you can play or sing along with the rhythm-only track. Songs include: Mele Kalikimaka (Merry Christmas to You) • We Wish You a Merry Christmas • Jingle Bells (with Hawaiian lyrics) • Angels We Have Heard on High • Away in a Manger • Deck the Halls • Hark! The Herald Angels Sing • Joy to the World • O Come, All Ye Faithful • Silent Night • Up on the Housetop • We Three Kings.
00000472 Book/CD Pack $19.95

FUN SONGS FOR UKULELE

50 terrific songs in standard notation and tablature for beginning to advanced ukulele players. Includes Hawaiian songs, popular standards, classic Western, Stephen Foster and more, with songs such as: The Darktown Strutters Ball • I'm Always Chasing Rainbows • Hot Lips • Gentle Annie • Maikai Waipio • Whispering • Ja-Da • China Boy • Colorado Trail • and many more. Also includes a chord chart and a special section on how to hold the ukulele.
00000407...$14.95

THE HAWAIIAN STEEL GUITAR AND ITS GREAT HAWAIIAN MUSICIANS

compiled & edited by Lorene Ruymar
This fascinating book takes a look at Hawaiian music; the origin of the steel guitar and how it spread throughout the world; Hawaiian playing styles, techniques and tunings; and more.
00000192 208 pages $34.95

UKULELE FOR COWBOYS

40 of your favorite cowboy songs in chords, standard notation and tab. Includes: Buffalo Gals • Night Herding Song • Doney Gal • Old Chisholm Trail • The Big Corral • Ragtime Cowboy Joe • Colorado Trail • Old Paint • Yellow Rose of Texas • Green Grow the Lilacs • and many more. Also includes a chord chart, historical background on many of the songs, and a short story on the history of the Hawaiian Cowboy.
00000408 ....$14.99

UKULELE SONGBOOK

compiled by Ron Middlebrook
This terrific collection for beginning to advanced ukulele players features easy arrangements of 50 great songs, in standard notation and tablature. Also teaches popular strum patterns, and how to tune the uke.
00000248 ....$9.95

UKULELE CHORDS
Plus Intros and Endings
by Ron Middlebrook
This handy chart includes clear, easy-to-see chord fingerings in all keys, plus a bonus section that provides favorite intros and endings in different keys. Also includes information on relative tuning.
00000246 ....$2.95

P.O. Box 17878 - Anaheim Hills, CA 92817
(714) 779-9390   www.centerstream-usa.com

More Great Guitar Books from Centerstream...